D1825384

THE BOOK OF FANTASTIC
BIRDS

Illustrated by
PETER BARRETT

Written by
JANE CARRUTH

octopus

CONTENTS

INTRODUCTION

Life without birds would be very dull indeed. There are almost nine thousand species of birds spread throughout the regions of the world. Many of them are so familiar that they are taken for granted. Others, like the birds in this book, are amazingly different from typical sparrows and robins.

In the tropical jungle-forests, there are birds so colourful that they dazzle the eye, and some so tiny that they could nest in the smallest of egg-cups. There are also birds taller and heavier than man and others that can jet-propel themselves out of the sky like thunderbolts.

It is strange to think that all these birds have ancestors that were reptiles. The story of their evolution goes back millions and millions of years to a creature called archaeopteryx whose fossilized remains have been discovered. It had a head, tail and teeth of a reptile, yet it was feathered and had wings like a bird.

In the course of evolution, some birds have disappeared altogether from the face of the earth. Others have lost their ability to fly. All surviving birds have had to adapt to their environment. In this book there is something fantastic about each bird described. It may be the manner of courtship or length of wingspan or just a practical matter of beaks and bills. In any case, the birds are grouped together according to their special features. To begin with, there are four birds with very unusual beaks. The next group of illustrations are very colourful, showing the vain Peacock, the Birds of Paradise and other exotic, tropical birds. Next follow four quite different types of birds that spend much of their time in or near water. And finally, there are three birds shown that are the largest of their kind, ending with the largest bird of all, the Ostrich.

Some words that may be unfamiliar are explained in the glossary at the back of this book.

ROSEATE SPOONBILL

Habitat: South America.
Size: 27–31 in.
It has a beak shaped like a spoon.

With its oddly shaped bill, which is not unlike a very long serving spoon, the Roseate Spoonbill is aptly named. These strange but beautiful birds range in colour from dark to palest pink and are found in South America. As they wade through the shallow waters, they scoop up shellfish and water insects with their broad flat bills that filter out any inedible matter. Like many waders, Spoonbills build platform nests of sticks on bushes or dwarf trees and return to the same nesting places yearly.

GREAT INDIAN
HORNBILL

Habitat: Jungle forests of Southern Asia.
Size: 45 in.
The female is sealed into the nest.

Another bird with a strange and very ungainly beak is the Great Indian Hornbill found in the jungle forests of India, Indonesia and Malaya, where its harsh, raucous call can be heard as night begins to fall.

Hornbills are quite unique in their nesting habits. When the female is ready to lay her eggs, she chooses a hole in a tree in which she conceals herself. The male then seals up the hole with mud leaving only a narrow slit through which he can feed her. Although a prisoner in her own nest, her eggs will be safe from marauding monkeys or snakes and she remains in her enclosure until her fledglings are a few months old. Then she breaks out and helps the cock to feed her hungry brood on the berries and insects which they eat in huge quantities.

SULPHUR BREASTED TOUCAN

Habitat: South American jungles.
Size: 21 in.
It has an enormous beak which is really very light.

Although the enormous beak of the gaudy Sulphur Breasted Toucan looks so heavy, it is really extremely light, being like a honeycomb inside. The Toucan uses it to reach out for berries which may be on a branch too slender to bear its weight. Sometimes it will toss the berries in the air and with a backward jerk of its head catch and swallow them in one gulp. Toucans live in tropical South American jungles where the brilliant flowers and fruits blend perfectly with their colourful feathers. But they take little advantage of this natural camouflage for they are perpetually announcing their presence with harsh, croaking cries that carry a long way.

SHOEBILL STORK
or WHALEHEAD

Habitat: East Africa.
Size: 48 in.
It sometimes performs a dance.

Like the Toucan, the Shoebill Stork puts its extraordinary bill to a very good use as it feeds among the papyrus swamps of the White Nile. With the hook at the tip of its broad bill, it digs out lung-fish buried in the mud. It also eats frogs, young turtles and even small crocodiles. Whaleheads, as Shoebills are sometimes called, build nests of sticks plastered with mud, and often decorate them with china, rags and even bones. They are solitary birds but if two or three do come together, they will break into an awkward kind of dance which they end with a little bow!

PEACOCK (male)

Habitat: India and Ceylon.
Size: 38–48 in., up to 90 in. in male with fully developed train.
He has a beautiful 'fan' of tail feathers.

The world is full of beautiful birds, but the proud and stately Peacock is rightly considered to be among the most beautiful. In ancient times, the Peacock was prized above all other birds and today he still commands admiration whenever he chooses to display his long train feathers in a shimmering jewel-like fan.

Peafowl are native to India and Ceylon where they live a sheltered and protected existence, but they have been domesticated all over the world.

The Peahen is smaller than the Peacock and quite plain in comparison. She lays about ten eggs in a nest which she has made on the ground. As soon as the chicks appear, she becomes a watchful and protective mother. Like so many other birds, whose breath-taking display of gorgeous feathers captures our imagination, the Peacock has a rasping scream which is most unpleasant to hear. The Peacock, in fact, is typical of many large birds who are easily seen. These birds have no song with which to woo their mates. Instead, they put on a display of eye-catching feathers.

VICTORIA CROWNED PIGEON

Habitat: New Guinea.
Size: 31 in.
It has a very beautiful crown.

The largest surviving member of the wild pigeon family, the Victoria Crowned Pigeon, has a special claim for recognition. Its fantastically beautiful crown, which has been compared by ornithologists to the texture of very fine lace, was considered to be as beautiful as Bird of Paradise feathers and was, at one time, greatly prized by traders.

Victoria Crowned Pigeons are gregarious and like to keep together whilst feeding on the ground. Unfortunately this habit made them fair game for hunters and their numbers have been steadily decreasing over the years. Now, like so many of the world's beautiful birds which are in danger of extinction, they are protected by law.

CROWNED CRANE

Habitat: Tropical Africa.
Size: 41 in.
**It performs a remarkable
acrobatic dance during
the mating season.**

The Crowned Crane of tropical
Africa is one of the most attractive
members of the crane family. Tall and
stately, it moves on slender legs among
the reeds and grasses bordering lakes or rivers.
Its distinctive crown sets it apart from its relatives
in Europe and America. All cranes, however, are
noted for their penetrating trumpet-like calls
that remind one of the French horn and for their
truly remarkable display of acrobatic dancing
during the mating season.
The hen lays two eggs in the year and the cock
assists in their incubation but only during day-
light hours. The tiny, newly hatched cranes
leave the nest on the same day they are born but
remain in their parents' care until they are about
six months old.
Cranes always fly in a V-formation with their
long necks extended. They migrate in
large flocks, soaring high above the
clouds in steady, graceful flight.

SAGE GROUSE (male)

Habitat: Western U.S.A.
Size: 22–27 in.
He inflates two distinctive air sacs during courtship.

Largest of the North American Grouse and the finest of all the western game-birds, the Sage Grouse is of particular interest for the remarkable display he stages during the courting season.

In the spring, the males come together in considerable numbers to go through an elaborate courtship ritual. To watch the Sage Grouse preparing to woo and win for himself a mate is an experience because he changes his appearance quite dramatically. This is done by spreading out his tail feathers and inflating two air sacs in front of his chest until they are the size of tennis balls! The resultant noise when he deflates these sacs is something between a grunt and a wheeze!

Game-birds are always in danger from man, but the Sage Grouse's patterned feathers blend in perfectly with the rolling sage of the high country of Colorado; and when he senses an enemy, he remains perfectly still. So, unlike the noisy Toucan, the Sage Grouse makes good use of the camouflage which nature has provided.

UMBRELLA BIRD (male)

Habitat: Central and South America.
Size: 19 in., lappet 13 in.
He has an umbrella-like crest of feathers on his head.

When the mating season comes round, male birds, in some way or another, try to attract females by display. Tropical birds are singularly well equipped to put on spectacular feather displays and none more so than the Umbrella Bird.
You can see from the picture the long lappet which hangs from his chest and which measures thirteen inches—almost, but not quite, as long as the rest of him. However, it is really the magnificent crest on his head which gives the Umbrella Bird his name. At the height of his courtship this wonderful crest opens out, umbrella-like, and covers the whole of his head. Umbrella Birds range from Costa Rica to Brazil and are typical of a family of perching birds known as Cotingas.

HUMMING BIRDS

Habitat: South America.
Size: Racket-tailed $4\frac{1}{2}$ in., Frilled Coquette $2\frac{3}{4}$ in.
They are the tiniest birds in the world.

Poets might well hesitate in their choice of words to describe the tiny and gorgeously arrayed Humming Birds. Apart from their minute size and jewel-like beauty, Humming Birds have other unique features. Their feet are so tiny that they cannot walk or hop, but they can fly backwards and forwards and hover to extract nectar from flowers. They build nests so small that they would fit into egg-cups and the vibration of their wings is so rapid that they produce a humming sound! Shown here are the Racket-tailed and the Frilled Coquette. The Racket-tailed is found in the Andes from Venezuela to Bolivia, and when courting, actually rubs its two long tail feathers together to make a rattling sound. The Frilled Coquette measures only $2\frac{3}{4}$ inches and is found in the jungles of Brazil.

QUETZAL (male)

Habitat: Rain forests of Mexico and Central America.
Size: 50 in., male's tail feathers may reach a length of 3 ft. or more.
Once worshipped by Aztecs and Mayas as the god of the air.

Only a relatively few birds have inspired men to worship them. The magnificent Quetzal, with his three foot long tail, is one. In ancient times, the Aztecs and Mayas worshipped the Quetzal as god of the air and reserved its colourful feathers for ceremonial purposes. Today, the people of Guatemala claim the Quetzal as their national bird, hailing it as a symbol of freedom. In fact, Quetzals rarely survive if taken into captivity. They build their nests high among the giant trees of the rain forests of Mexico and Central America, and both parents help to incubate the eggs. But when the cock takes his turn, he faces outwards, his wonderful tail feathers curving forward over his back. Quetzals are members of the colourful Trogon family that live in tropical forests.

PRINCE RUDOLPH'S BLUE BIRD OF PARADISE (male)

Habitat: Tropical forests of New Guinea.
Size: 11 in.
He hangs upside down and sings.

It is said that when the 16th century Portuguese explorer, Ferdinand Magellan, sailed westwards through the Atlantic and Pacific, one of the many things he saw for the first time was a beautiful bird which he described in such glowing terms that it was named 'Bird of Paradise'.

Prince Rudolph's Blue Bird of Paradise is one of the most strikingly beautiful of the Family Paradisaeidae. During the courting season, the male hangs upside down from his perch so that the female may admire the beautiful ripples of colour as he vibrates his plumes. At the same time, he sings in a low voice, all on the same note, with head tilted to one side. He will keep this up for ten or fifteen minutes at a time.

Birds of Paradise are natives of the tropical forests of New Guinea and the adjoining islands. They feed mostly on insects and fruit.

PERUVIAN
COCK-OF-THE-ROCK (male)

Habitat: Andes, Columbia and Peru.
Size: 15 in.
He does an acrobatic dance.

This is an exciting bird—with its rich red plumage and large handsome crest that hides its beak. Like the Umbrella Bird, the Cock-of-the-Rock is a member of the Cotinga family and he, too, puts on a spectacular display of acrobatics during the courtship season.

Found in rocky ravines near mountain streams in the Andes and in Columbia and Peru, the Cock-of-the-Rock is gregarious and sociable. Even his courting is done in the company of other males who gather together in a clearing in the forest. Their dancing and hopping is very energetic but, every now and then, the dancing stops and the birds take up a stationary pose in the manner of children playing a game of statues!

SUPERB BIRD
OF PARADISE (male)

Habitat: Forests of southeast New Guinea.
Size: 9 in.
He fans out his beautiful feathers in a frill.

Male birds who make much of their feathers in display are often much more dazzling than their prospective partners. This is particularly evident in the Birds of Paradise for the hens are always dull and inconspicuous. In courtship, the Superb Bird of Paradise makes skilful use of his brightly coloured feathers by fanning them out in an eye-catching frill.

Displays such as this nearly led to the extinction of Birds of Paradise. Their plumes were so much in demand by ladies for hats that thousands were killed and laws had to be introduced to protect these birds.

KING OF SAXONY
BIRD OF PARADISE (male)

Habitat: Central mountain ranges of New Guinea.
Size: $8\frac{3}{4}$ in.
He performs a fantastic ritual during courtship.

This delicate, robin-like Bird of Paradise is rarely seen because he is hidden away high up in the central mountain ranges of New Guinea. At the start of his courtship, he calls the female to his display ground by a loud hissing noise. When she comes, he begins to bounce up and down on his perch, hissing all the time. Then the long head plumes sweep forward until, at last, they are almost touching the advancing hen. So well concealed are these special places in the forests where this ritual dance occurs that only a very few privileged people have ever come across them.

MAGNIFICENT FRIGATE BIRD (male)

Habitat: Tropical Atlantic and Pacific coasts of America.
Size: 36–39 in.
It is the fastest flying sea bird.

The Magnificent Frigate Bird lives up to its name in the mating season when he displays a huge, bright red, balloon-like pouch under his chin to attract the female.

They are the fastest of the flying sea birds with a wing-span of around seven feet, and they are tough, belligerent pirates when it comes to food snatching. With patient cunning, they lie in wait for other birds to do their fishing for them and then bully them into giving up their catch as they land.

For this reason, they are sometimes given the name Man-o'-war.

GREATER BIRD OF PARADISE (male)

Habitat: Lowlands, up to 3,000 ft.
on Aru Islands and South New Guinea.
Size: male 17–18 in.
He does an extraordinary ritual dance.

This extremely beautiful bird found on the Aru Islands and New Guinea was the first of the Birds of Paradise to be introduced to the Western world. Much has been written about his extraordinary ritual dance which usually takes place when no females are present.

In the mating season, a dozen or more of these male birds select certain trees and perch on the branches in preparation for their dance. They begin by giving loud ear-splitting cries that travel a surprising distance. Then each member of the party commences a slow dance along the branch of a tree. With head bowed and body swaying from side to side, the Greater Bird of Paradise is totally absorbed. As the dance increases in intensity, the bird fans out his long silky plumes over his back.

The climax is reached without warning. Suddenly, the dancer bends his head so that he hangs down underneath the perch, wings spread out over his back, as shown in the picture. In company with his other fellow performers, he will remain in this position for several minutes.

Ornithologists are at a loss to explain why such an elaborate ritual dance should be performed when there are no females to witness it. But some say that it may be entirely symbolic and merely a prelude to mating.

MANDARIN DUCK (drake)

Habitat: China and Japan.
Size: 16½ in.
It has the most brilliant colouring of all fresh-water ducks.

The attractive Mandarin Duck of China and Japan belongs to the large family of perching ducks that can boast of having the most brilliant colouring of all fresh-water ducks.

Mandarin Ducks live in forests and make their nests in trees, and if you look at the Mandarin Duck closely you will see the strong claws on its webbed feet that enable it to cling to the tree trunks.

The Chinese are particularly fond of these ornamental waterfowl and breed them in captivity. In courtship, the drakes whistle and grunt as they display their feathers with movements of their head, wings and tail. Both parents help to incubate the eggs and because of the affection they show to each other, the Chinese say that the Mandarin Duck is a symbol of fidelity in marriage!

BLUE-FOOTED BOOBY

Habitat: Tropical Eastern
Pacific and Galapagos Islands.
Size: 34 in.
**They dive-bomb
into the sea to catch fish.**

This sea bird of the eastern Pacific and the Galapagos Islands with its long
beak and webbed blue feet was, it is said, given its name by the Spaniards.
'Bobo' is the Spanish for fool, and the Boobies seemed to go out of their
way to earn it by allowing sailors to catch them almost without effort!
Boobies are renowned for the manner in which they fish. Vast numbers of
them dive-bomb out of the sky into the sea in a most spectacular fashion.
Blue-footed Boobies belong to the family Sulidae, and the females lay
only one egg which they cover with their feet.

ROCKHOPPER PENGUIN

Habitat: Islands of the southern oceans.
Size: 27 in.
They bray like donkeys.

Penguins, like Boobies are expert fishers. Nesting on the islands of the southern oceans, these flightless Rockhopper Penguins make long sea journeys during the year, but return to their nesting ground in early spring where, on the beaches, they lay their eggs.

All Penguins have a comical air about them, and the Rockhoppers are no exception. They are at their funniest during courtship when, with loud and persistent donkey-like braying, they set out to impress the ladies.

FLAMINGO

Habitat: Southern France, South America, Bahamas,
East Africa and India.
Size: 60 in.
It uses its special bill as a sieve.

There are three different species of Flamingo but the Common or Greater Flamingo with its rose- coloured feathers is the most beautiful of all. In the South of France these long-legged birds have built huge colonies on the mud-flats. They are found, too, in South America, the Bahamas, East Africa and India. Their honking cry as they take to the air resembles that of a goose; but when they are at rest on the water, they look more like giant pink swans. The Flamingo feeds in a unique way—it literally turns its head upside down so that the top of its bill, which is lid-shaped, scoops up the muddy water containing its food. The reject material is then filtered out. Flamingos use their specialised bills to build cone-shaped nests of mud in which the female lays a single egg. After the chick is hatched, the mother takes it along to a communal nursery run by the parents of the colony.

ANDEAN CONDOR

Habitat: Andes at heights of 6,000–18,000 ft.
Size: 39 in., wing-span up to almost 10 ft.
It has the largest wing-span of any living bird.

The great Andean Condor, with a wing-span of nearly 10 feet, is an impressive but scarcely attractive bird. The heaviest bird of prey in the New World, and an expert at gliding, it is most frequently seen in countries like Chile and Peru where it nests on lonely mountain ledges.

Like all vultures, these awesome birds of prey search out carrion (the bodies of dead animals) on which to feed—though they will also swoop down on live game. Despite its size and weight, the Andean Condor is capable of dropping out of the sky at tremendous speed; and guided by its exceptionally keen eyesight, it rarely misses a kill. Generally speaking, the head, throat and lower legs of vultures are without feathers and you can see from the picture that this is true of the Andean Condor.

Like falcons and eagles, the female chooses a rocky ledge for her nest where she lays two brown-spotted, yellowish eggs. Her fledglings are slow to develop and it is eight to ten weeks before they can leave the nest.

There are records which seem to prove that Andean Condors live to a ripe old age—in the region of 65 years, which is unusually long for a bird.

EAGLE OWL

Habitat: Mountain forests of Europe.
Size: 27 in.
It has been known to live for up to 68 years.

Another bird of prey and the biggest of its kind
is the Eagle Owl with its tufted ears.
Silent in flight, the Eagle Owl is an expert
hunter, feeding on snakes, rabbits and other
rodents. It hunts just as darkness begins to fall
and its eerie hooting and sometimes unearthly
moaning can be very frightening to those who
unknowingly hear the owl for the first time.
In the daytime, it will perch motionless on
some rock or tree—almost invisible against
its natural background—and with eyes
half-shut as if in sleep. But let something
unusual stir in the undergrowth and it
is instantly alert. The female lays
her round white eggs in the
spring and when they hatch,
both parents help to raise
the new little family of two
or three fledglings.

OSTRICH

Habitat: Deserts and savannas of Africa.
Size: 8 ft., weight 300 lbs.
It is the largest living bird.

The biggest living bird of all is the Ostrich. Eight feet tall and weighing up to 300 lbs. or more, Ostriches are among the running birds of the deserts and the grassy plains called savannas. To compensate for their inability to fly, they have long, powerful legs which carry them over the ground at speeds of twenty to thirty miles an hour.
In the mating season, the cock becomes dangerous and aggressive, using his powerful legs effectively as weapons.

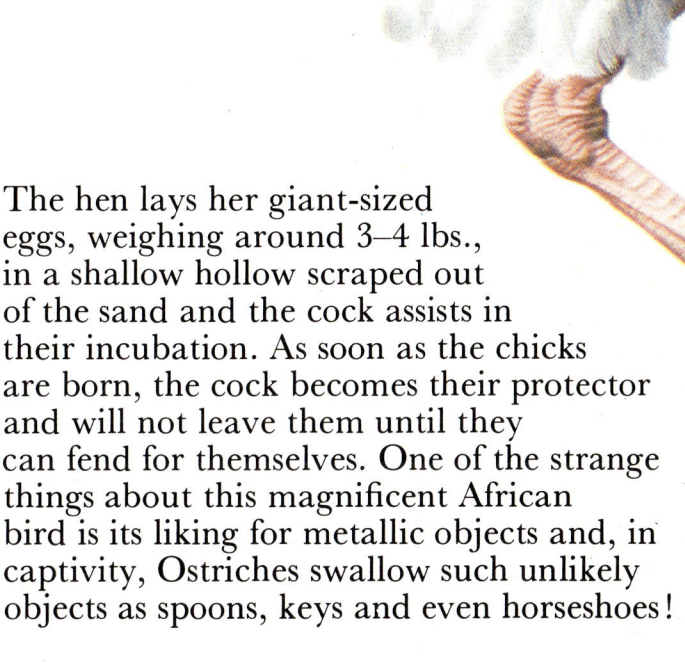

The hen lays her giant-sized eggs, weighing around 3–4 lbs., in a shallow hollow scraped out of the sand and the cock assists in their incubation. As soon as the chicks are born, the cock becomes their protector and will not leave them until they can fend for themselves. One of the strange things about this magnificent African bird is its liking for metallic objects and, in captivity, Ostriches swallow such unlikely objects as spoons, keys and even horseshoes!

GLOSSARY

archeopteryx: the oldest known bird (fossil).

bill: a bird's beak.

carrion: dead flesh.

cock: male bird.

crown: top part of head.

drake: male duck.

evolution: the gradual process of development of animal life, from the earliest species onwards.

fledgling: young bird.

flock: number of birds, feeding or travelling together.

hen: female fowl.

incubate: to hatch eggs by sitting on them.

lappet: flap of flesh.

migrate: move from one place to another.

ornithologist: person who studies birds.

plume: feather.

reptile: cold-blooded, egg-laying, scaly-skinned animal.

Planned and directed by The Archon Press Limited, 14-18 Ham Yard, London W1
First published 1975 by Octopus Books Limited, 59 Grosvenor Street, London W1

ISBN 0 7064 0335 5

© 1974 The Archon Press Ltd

Distributed in Australia by Rigby Limited
30 North Terrace, Kent Town, Adelaide, South Australia 5067

Printed in Italy
by Stabilimento Grafico Editoriale
Fratelli Spada - Ciampino-Roma